STEGOSAURUS would slam its tail on the ground to warn off other dinosaurs.

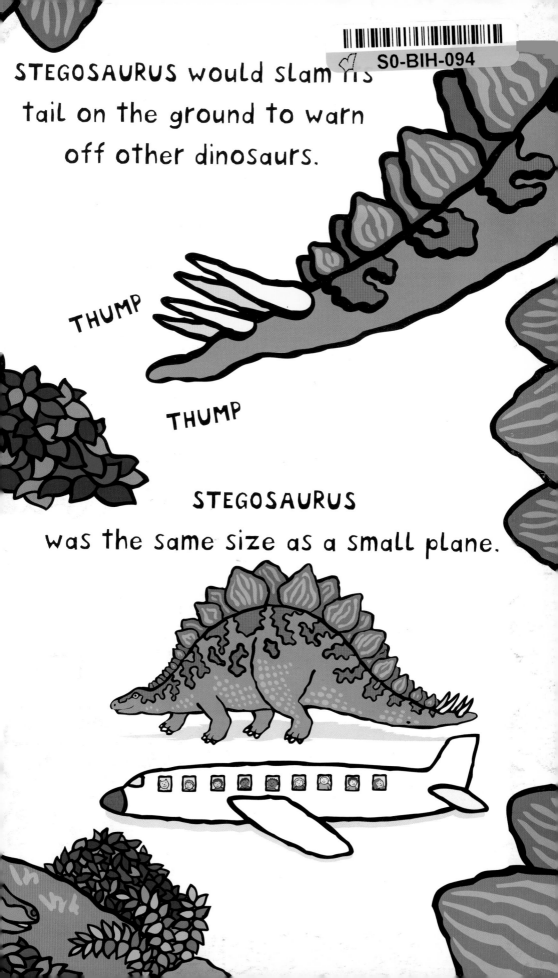

THUMP

THUMP

STEGOSAURUS was the same size as a small plane.

PTERODACTYLUS

TER-<u>OH</u>-DAK-<u>TI</u>-LUS

The PTERODACTYLUS was a winged reptile that could fly. It had little fingers attached to its wings to help it eat its food.

PTERODACTYLUS could fly long distances because it had very light bones.

The adult PTERODACTYLUS
laid eggs, just like birds
do today.

PTERODACTYLUS lived near lakes.
Its long, pointed beak and small
teeth helped it catch fish.

BRACHIOSAURUS
BRAK-EE-OH-SAW-RUS

BRACHIOSAURUS was one of the biggest dinosaurs that ever lived.

BRACHIOSAURUS was as long as three buses and weighed as much as twenty elephants.

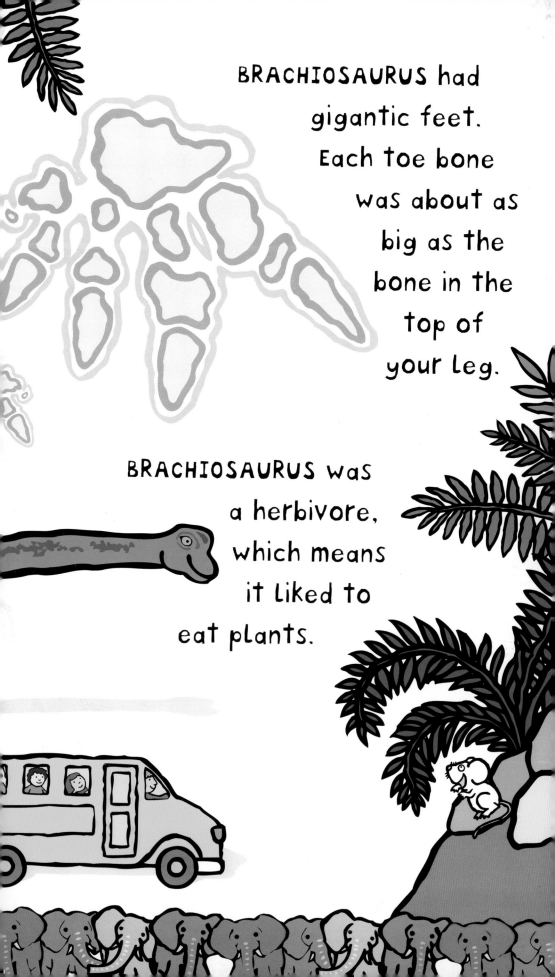

BRACHIOSAURUS had gigantic feet. Each toe bone was about as big as the bone in the top of your leg.

BRACHIOSAURUS was a herbivore, which means it liked to eat plants.

TYRANNOSAURUS REX
TIE-RAN-OH-SAW-RUS REX

TYRANNOSAURUS REX was a dinosaur that liked to eat other dinosaurs.

SNIFF

SNIFF

TYRANNOSAURUS REX had a strong sense of smell and good eyesight, which helped it find its food easily.

TYRANNOSAURUS REX
Left huge footprints.

TYRANNOSAURUS REX
had a huge head,
strong jaws, and
sharp teeth.

GNASH
GNASH

Each tooth was the
size of a banana.

TRICERATOPS
TRY-<u>SER</u>-AH-<u>TOPS</u>

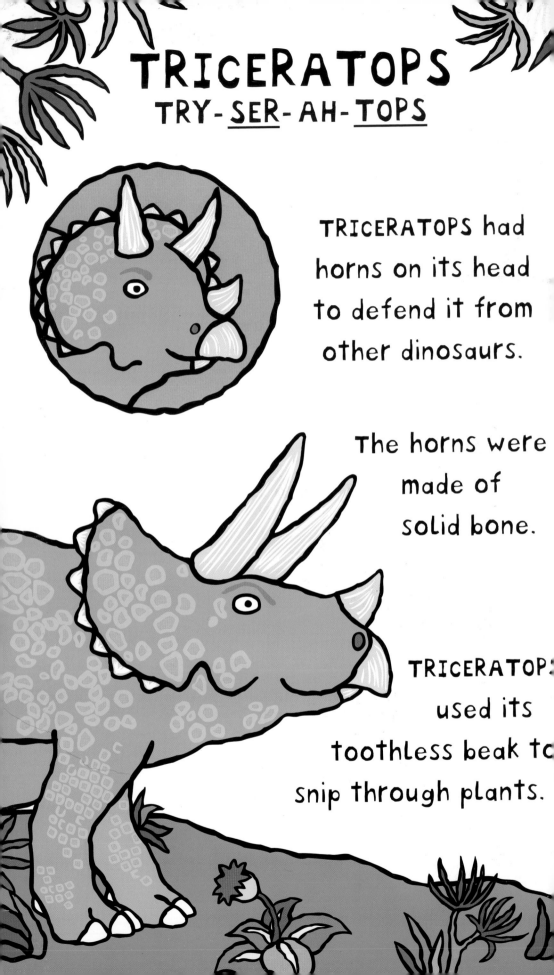

TRICERATOPS had horns on its head to defend it from other dinosaurs.

The horns were made of solid bone.

TRICERATOPS used its toothless beak to snip through plants.